Marylou Faure

Counter-Print Books

Marylou Faure

Style is something many spend a career chasing. An aesthetic, an unconventional approach or a way of thinking, it's that elusive element that gives a portfolio distinction in an overcrowded visual world. Some do achieve it, however, it can be derivative, piggy-backing on something that's come before them. A unique style that's truly distinctive, therefore, is hard to come by. But it's something Marylou Faure has in abundance.

A Parisian illustrator now based in London, Marylou's work is the type you can recognise a mile off. Flat, block colours form graphic shapes in her compositions, spliced by thick black and white lines carving objects and figures out of negative space. Pulling focus in each work: one or several women, Marylou's signature character and the element which has helped to make her portfolio so iconic in such a short space of time.

Bold, colourful, graphic, playful and quirky are the words she responds with when asked to describe her work. When first embarking on her illustration career, this singular visual language was one she had her sights firmly set on. "The only thing I started establishing early on in my career, is that I wanted my work to be representative of my character," she tells me, as we chat. "I wanted to have something that felt modern and fresh and so I quickly made my work more graphic; simple, with thick lines, few colours and fewer details."

"You need to feel confident about your work as an artist, and it's easier when you have a clear notion of what your style is and what the qualities of your work are."

Having set out with such clear aesthetic intentions, it's an approach which has stuck and developed over the years. "You need to feel confident about your work as an artist, and it's easier when you have a clear notion of what your style is and what the qualities of your work are," Marylou adds when asked why she was so propelled towards defining her work in this way. "It's already hard to fight against impostor syndrome as an illustrator, but if my work was going in every direction, I would feel less confident selling it and justifying what I do."

While Marylou embarked on her career in illustration in 2015, her creative interests stem from a young age, and she grew up in a creative household. Her mum is an artist and, when they were young,

coaxed Marylou and her sisters into trying every artistic medium they could get their hands on. "I liked it straight away," she recalls, "we did loads of drawing classes, painting classes – I went to the museums a lot." This interest was further nurtured by her dad, a keen photographer who introduced her to the practice as a teenager. A stimulating upbringing, it made choosing a path easy for Marylou. "I always knew I wanted to go into the industry," she adds.

Marylou's childhood was spent between London and Paris. Originally from the French capital, Marylou lived in London between the ages of four and fourteen. The lure of the city which always felt like a second home remained, however, and after meeting her boyfriend during a six-month stint in Bournemouth as an exchange student, it made sense to make the move after graduating from ESAG Penninghen. A school specialising in graphic design and art direction, its ambitious environment wasn't suited to Marylou's outlook on creativity. "It was a pretty hard school that was all about competition and, not only doing well, but doing better than the others," she explains. "I didn't like that, but it definitely toughened me up to start in the industry."

Moving to London post-graduation was instrumental in Marylou becoming an illustrator as, before settling in the city, her understanding of the medium and its potential was more than lacking. What she discovered was a thriving illustration community full of creatives challenging the very notion of the medium, but also a city which, in itself, inspired her. It's a story which mimics that of renowned illustrator Malika Favre, who coincidentally was one of the very people who Marylou found so inspiring. "I realised that you can be graphic with illustration, that it can be very broad – it doesn't have to be targeted towards children or anything like that. So I had a bit of an eye-opening at that point," she recalls. Alongside Malika, it was the work of Hattie Stewart, and Parra (among many others) which had, and continues to have, "the biggest influence on my choices."

Upon first arriving in the city, Marylou undertook several internships before starting to work at a creative agency called Nice and Serious. Based in southeast London (and with an office in New York), it's an agency which works on projects that have a positive impact on society – an approach which Marylou has carried with her over the years. As her interests strayed from graphic design to illustration, Marylou continued to work for the creative agency on a part-time basis. This, coupled with the support of the wider creative community in London, meant Marylou's career ascended quickly. "I love the atmosphere in London," she adds as we discuss the like-mindedness she has found there. "I feel like it's very inclusive and that people aren't out to get one another. There are so many collaborative projects, collectives and, when I started, it helped me meet people in the industry and discover other people's work."

"I'm not a patient person. As soon as I have an idea in my mind, I have to work on it until it's done."

"I think anyone who feels good in their body looks beautiful and is confident and that's what I aim for people to feel when they look at my characters."

All this being said, it was Marylou's portfolio and drive to achieve which did the most work. Once her mind was made up, she did not waver. "I'm not a patient person," she says, laughing. "As soon as I have an idea in my mind, I have to work on it until it's done." While adding that this is something she is working on, it most certainly contributed to her success early on, and the development of her style. "Unconsciously, I do think it was a contributing factor as to why I developed my style in a certain way," she muses. "Having that satisfaction of your work being done, and being able to show it around as quickly as possible – that's what I like." In turn, a day's work often finishes late for Marylou, who works from home alongside her husband (and their whippet, Charlie).

When creating a work, she always starts with a rough sketch in a notebook, which will form the basis of the idea and composition. Then, she moves to her iPad, creating a cleaner version of that sketch where all the details are added. "This is the longest part of the process because it's really where the balance and composition need to be on point," she explains. "I add the black shapes, which helps me create the contrast I want, and I'll play around with echoing elements, parts breaking out of shapes and some contrast between sharp and round lines." Finally, it's time to colour, "and if the sketch is done right," this doesn't take long at all.

This specific process is what informs Marylou's style and it's a rigid one she doesn't deviate from, imposing certain parameters on herself within which her images emerge. Firstly, there's the notion of elements echoing or merging to produce a congruous arrangement. This could mean a protagonist's hair mirroring the clouds behind her, her nails taking the same shape as the centre of a flower, or the bun on top of her head replicating her own nipples. Including repetition within an image like this, "makes the work feel more united" and the shapes "in harmony with one another." These well-balanced elements are then juxtaposed with opposing forms to create contrast, retaining a sense of the unexpected in the work and ensuring a certain strength and prominence.

Over the years, Marylou's striking work has appeared on everything from posters to campaigns to skateboards and murals, and for clients including Spotify, Nike, YouTube, Apple, MTV, ASOS and Deliveroo (the list goes on). As a creative, she's restless and explorative, always excited by the next thing; it's what she loves about illustration. "An illustration can become pretty much anything, which is exciting," she tells me. "It's nice to see your work live differently." It's this wide-ranging practice which instils a whimsical playfulness in Marylou's portfolio.

While collaborating with such an impressive client list, it's remarkable that Marylou also keeps up an avid self-initiated practice. It's here where her passion for her medium shines, taking on briefs which have a strong social or ethical cause. It's something which stems from her time as a graphic designer at Nice and Serious: "When I went freelance, I got bored quickly of the projects I didn't believe in." So she began working with charities and nonprofits, or entering open calls for work promoting sustainability or International Women's Day, for example, and it quickly became a core part of her portfolio.

> "If I'm using my work to support brands to make more money, I'd like to also use my work to support charities."

"I like to take a bit of time to work on projects where it's purely about raising money for a charity that I like and that I support. If I'm using my work to support brands to make more money, I'd like to also use my work to support charities."

But with Marylou, none of this is forced – everything happens naturally and altruistically. A prominent theme in her work is the advocacy of equal rights for all and a strong representation of women,

but it wasn't necessarily a conscious decision. "I try to be a positive person in my everyday life and having body confidence meant a lot, and I wanted to represent that," she says of her move to include female characters in all of her work. "But I didn't choose to only draw women, that was just what I wanted to represent all of the time." In turn, Marylou's work is a true product of her personality, it's authentic and genuine, and she couldn't do it any other way – even if she wanted to.

> "I feel very close to what I do and I think that's why I started illustrating women. There's a lot of therapy in my work."

It would be remiss not to spend some time looking at these female characters that form so much of Marylou's work. While they always have a similar aesthetic, through composition and careful cropping, she conveys myriad qualities of femininity, be that playfulness, sensuality, strength or innocence. Without eyes to express such emotions, she cleverly employs body language and positioning to portray a mood. The results, in their own quiet way, challenge notions of beauty and femininity.

"I think anyone who feels good in their body looks beautiful and is confident," she says, "and that's what I aim for people to feel when they look at my characters. And even though my women have a certain body type and they have some 'cliché' aspects of femininity to them, that's just my aesthetic and it shouldn't mean there aren't other ways of being feminine and beautiful. I don't look like them, but I can still relate to the way they feel."

The women Marylou draws are also a way for her to channel her ambitions. "I feel very close to what I do and I think that's why I started illustrating women," she analyses. "There's a lot of therapy in my work. My characters are very confident and they don't care about what people think of them. They have qualities that I aspire to have more of."

Ultimately, therefore, how Marylou's characters look has nothing to do with it. It is the attitude they exude that matters. They are unapologetic and they don't take themselves too seriously which is why, when asked what she wants people to take from her work, Marylou concludes: "A bit of fun and playfulness, mostly. And positivity."

Ruby Boddington

Marylou Faure

———

The Female Body

"I think there's something about the attitude, the confidence and the sensuality of my characters that makes me go back to drawing them – it's something quite personal, where they represent a sense of freedom and state of mind that I think everyone should aim to have."

I've always been drawn to the representation of the female body, even when I was a little girl. I used to spend hours looking at comic strips, manga, photos or movies that had a female character that was represented in a powerful way. I found it so inspiring. There was something about their confidence that drew me to them, maybe because I felt a bit insecure growing up and watching them gave me some of their strength.

I think I noticed quite early on that there was a problem with the way women were being talked about, how they were represented and in some of the worst cases, how they were treated. So that theme in my drawing started quite early on, from when I was a teenager, when my focus was having my own interpretation of how women should be represented.

"There's more freedom in nudity, it makes my work feel personal and intimate. When my characters have clothing on, they seem less interesting to me."

As for the work I do now, I think there's something about the attitude, the confidence and the sensuality of my characters that makes me go back to drawing them – it's something quite personal, where they represent a sense of freedom and state of mind that I think everyone should aim to have.

The nudes, in particular, that I create have an inherent freedom that makes my work feel more personal and intimate. When my characters have clothing on, they seem less interesting to me. I think the fact that they are naked makes me draw them in a different way. I feel I draw them more naturally. Nudity is also a way to play around with the body shapes in a more organic way.

I find the human body very graphic, a bit like nature you can really use it as a source of inspiration. I hope I'll never get bored of the human form and that it continues to inspire me as much as the women that I depict.

My subjects aren't anyone in particular, but they all have the same qualities like confidence, sensuality, strength and a sense of playfulness to them. In a way, the characters I portray are, inevitably, a reflection of myself. My work is so personal and it is strongly representative of my state of mind and the mood I was in while creating it. My characters are, in fact, very often lost in their own heads, daydreaming, which is something that I do a lot. So in this sense, I can see myself through them, in their poses and attitude. But I also have a feeling of being

more of a spectator, or a creator, than an actual character. They sometimes represent my feelings but, ultimately, I'm not them, they are more of an aspect than an actual representation of myself.

"Confident and unapologetic women certainly inspire me. Women that aren't afraid to be both talented, smart, funny, caring and feeling good within their bodies."

I'm really interested in the way an artwork can make you feel, and it's partly the reason why I wanted to become an artist. That's the main inspiration behind why I represent the people in my work the way that I do. It's really more about what they embody and how they feel, rather than what they look like.

Confident and unapologetic women certainly inspire me. Women that aren't afraid to be both talented, smart, funny, caring and feeling good within their bodies. I'm pulled towards those who are careless and free in the way they handle themselves, without thinking they shouldn't be this way. I find inspiration in those who aren't afraid of going against clichés and the women in my life, my mum and sisters, inspire me simply by being the kindest people I know.

In terms of role models, artists such as Grace Jones, Etta James, Khatia Buniatishvili, Yayoi Kusama or Dora Maar are incredibly inspiring, both for their talent and what they've achieved.

"There's definitely a big role to be played by individuals, brands and media to make sure that there's an accurate representation of what young girls can aspire to become."

There are many female role models but the problem is that you sometimes have to search for them. There are so many talented women out there who simply haven't been put in the spotlight. In terms of my professional life, I have been pretty sheltered from this, as I feel like in my field of work, and as a creative working for myself, I've never been held back as a woman. If anything, most of the illustrators I look up to are women. It's a very important and current cause to fight for. There's definitely a big role to be played by individuals, brands and the media to make sure that there's an accurate representation of what young girls can aspire to become. I hope my work can add to this conversation in a small way.

The idea behind my work is to show
people that being confident can give
you a sense of empowerment. I always
try to present my female characters in
a similar way — as strong and feminine,
in the hope that some of their qualities
will reflect on me, as well as my audience.
My characters never care about what
other people think about them and
neither should we.

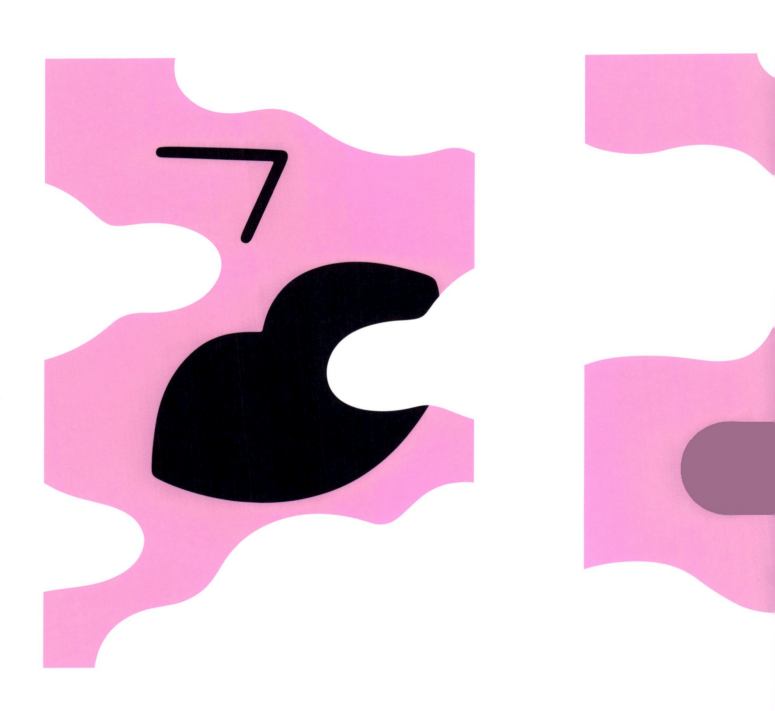

The Female Body

Blossom
Illustration series for Faure's
solo exhibition with art
gallery Woodbury House,
in collaboration with Nicce.

Marylou Faure

22

The Female Body

Having my characters being nude allows me to play around with the raw shapes of the body. It means I can fully represent its curviness and sensuality and give my characters the attitude I want them to portray.

Intimacy
Illustration series depicting female characters in an intimate moment.

 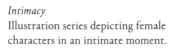

The Female Body

Posterzine
Cover design for a zine
collaboration with Posterzine
featuring Faure's work
and interview.

Hairband
Screen print design for Faure's
online shop.

The Female Body

Dreamy
Series of illustrations representing
a state of calm and peacefulness.

My characters are often daydreaming and lost in their own head. It's a theme I love to explore throughout my work — partly because it's something that I do myself a lot — but also because there is something quite mysterious and attractive about someone ignoring the outside world and taking a break from anything happening around them.

The Female Body

Marylou Faure

—

Aesthetics & Compositions

"I enjoy experimentation and working on something that's a bit different to what I usually do, while still keeping the core values of my aesthetic. This way, my work is given the freedom to constantly grow and mature."

I've always loved drawing, but I actually wanted to become an animator for a long time. Movies and animations were such a big part of my childhood that it made me want to work in the industry. I started my studies at Penninghen, in France and my plan was to stay there a couple of years and then try to enter Les Gobelins to start an animation course.

But in the meantime, I did a six month Erasmus in Bournemouth, where I studied animation and it made me realise I didn't have the patience to work in motion design. I'm actually a very impatient person and what I love about my work now is that I can start and finish a piece in a very short time.

Something that really attracted me to illustration was when I moved to London in 2012, where I discovered the work of illustrators that I fell in love with. It made me realise that illustration could be very modern and graphic, which wasn't the view I had of it when I was studying.

When I was studying illustration in Paris, the work I did was very different. It was mainly black and white, very detailed with thin lines – my drawings were much darker and a little creepy. It was only for my Master's project that I started playing around with colours and injecting more colour in my work.

"The sketching phase is the most important and takes the longest time. If I try to move on to colour when the sketch isn't perfect, it will always lead to a difficult artwork to finish."

Later, when I began working as an in-house designer at an agency, I started trying to develop an illustrative style that I was happy with during my spare time. My aim was to be able to work freelance as soon as I felt confident enough. This was the inception of my style as you see it now. I would say it started to develop then and has kept evolving through the years.

I enjoy experimentation and working on something that's a bit different to what I usually do, while still keeping the core values of my aesthetic. This way, my work is given the freedom to constantly grow and mature.

My process is usually the same with each brief. I'll always start with a very rough sketch in my notebook – it will be pretty small and will just help conceptualise the idea and composition. I'll then work on a cleaner version of that sketch on my iPad and I will add the black shapes. This really helps to create the contrast and defines

where the black and white will be. Even though my work is very colourful, black and white are the primary focus and their shape will define the artwork.

The sketching phase is the most important and takes the longest time. If I try to move on to colour when the sketch isn't perfect, it will always lead to a difficult artwork to finish. Sketching is also the moment where I will try to add some details, or 'winks' as we say in French, where I'll play around with shapes that are echoing or contrasting one another. It's a very fun process and my favourite part.

"As I developed my style, I knew I wanted colour to be central to my work and I wanted it to be very bright and positive."

I really used to be terrible with associating colours. That's the main reason why I would primarily use black or white. As I developed my style, I knew I wanted colour to be central to my work and I wanted it to be very bright and positive. I started playing around with different colour palettes – I tried and failed with a lot of them and then I tried a new one for a personal project and it felt right. Since then the colours have changed a bit but they will always be very vibrant and there will always be a pink or a red in there.

Inspiration doesn't always strike when you want or force it to. I have periods where I know there's no point in trying to draw anything personal – because I don't feel particularly inspired. I used to really fight against this and force myself to think of a new theme or idea for a series, but I've learnt that it doesn't work. Now, when I don't feel like drawing anything new, I don't. Instead I use my time doing other things like reading, walking, going to exhibitions or travelling. It helps my mind to take a break and I always have a very productive phase after that.

Inspiration can often come from unlikely sources – people, moods, conversations, jokes or songs. I feel like they all stay in the back of my mind and often help with new sketches later on. I find photography and music incredibly inspiring, especially when working on new themes. I sometimes base my personal series on names of songs that have inspired me, and listening to them will really give me ideas for content.

It all comes together to help create a style that is hopefully vibrant, colourful, playful, graphic, female-focussed and, above all, fun.

Daydream
Illustration series for Faure's solo
exhibition with art gallery Hen's
Teeth, based in Dublin.

DAYDREAM

DAYDREAM

Sketches
Examples of sketches
from different artworks.

I like my sketches to be extremely clean and precise — almost like a final piece of art itself. I find it really satisfying and it really gives me an accurate idea of whether or not the artwork will be strong or not. It's the step where everything is being put into place — the shapes, the contrast, the patterns and the balance of the artwork.

Stella Artois
Series of illustrations made during the 2020 Australian Open, representing the mood and atmosphere of the event. Each piece was printed and showcased at the Stella Artois exhibition hall at the OA.

Marylou Faure

Samsung was a fun project to work on —
I had a lot of creative freedom and it was
a good exercise to work on a different
format. Creating an artwork for a
wallpaper means you have to leave some
space for the apps to live in and put the
focus of the illustration in the right area.

Samsung
Client project made for Samsung —
series of wallpapers to be used
on their different devices.

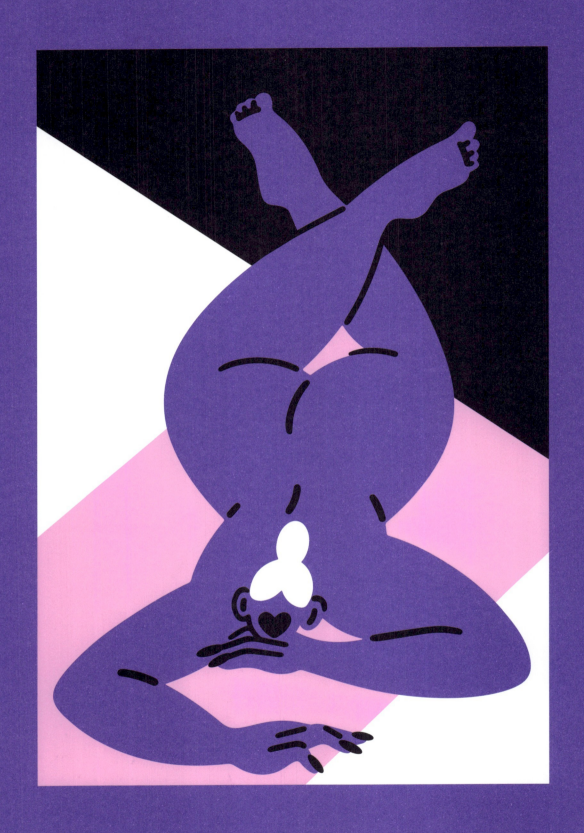

Ski
Personal series about travel
and skiing.

Travelling or taking a break from work is when I can refuel in inspiration and creativity. The act of doing nothing helps me find the motivation and energy to work on something new later on. And there's nothing I love more than chilling near the poolside, so I naturally did a series that reflected that feeling.

A la Piscine
Illustration series for Faure's solo exhibition at The Book Club, a series that aims to bring you back to your last sunny days chilling by the pool.

Aesthetics & Compositions

Marylou Faure

Marylou Faure

91

Marylou Faure

———

Artistic Voice

"If your work has a message behind it, then you can definitely make an impact with a wide audience. Whether it's by collaborating with charities and the projects you believe in, or conveying your own convictions through the work you do for clients."

My passion for cause-driven work started when I left the agency I was working for, who specialised in projects around sustainability, environmental and social issues. I was suddenly working freelance on projects that weren't talking about any of the issues I cared about. I missed it from the beginning and wanted to steer my work towards projects that had a stronger message at their core.

So, I started taking part in pro bono projects which invited artists to respond to a particular cause or issue. This led me to working on some of the artwork I'm the most proud of.

> "My work is very personal, so if something is happening in the world that is making me feel or think a certain way, it will translate through my work."

Having women as the focus of my work also gradually led me to take part in projects that were fighting for women's rights. It wasn't something I thought about when working on developing my style, it happened naturally and I'm so glad it did.

My work is very personal, so if something is happening in the world that is making me feel or think a certain way, it will translate through my work. That being said, I actually don't see my work as being particularly political – mainly because the first thing I want people to get out of it is a sense of playfulness and fun. I sometimes am responding to what's happening in the world, but my main goal is to distract and entertain.

I feel like it's such a great time to work in this industry. Illustration is really valued at the moment and utilised in so many different ways. If your work has a message behind it, then you can definitely make an impact with a wide audience. Whether it's by collaborating with charities and the projects you believe in, or conveying your own convictions through the work you do for clients. Personally, the cause I'm most interested in is representing women in my own way by adding more diversity in my characters and their relationships.

My hope is that my work brings a bit of joy and positivity to the people who view it. I hope they find it playful and entertaining. I often see people tagging their friends or partner on my post, and since my work is pretty cheeky, I hope it's a bit of an inside joke and something that will make them smile.

Being an illustrator, we are often given the platform of expression through talks and workshops. This is something I both love and hate but can be very rewarding. I can't stress enough how anxious I am the weeks and days before I do a talk, but I also love the adrenaline and the feeling of achievement from pushing myself outside of my normal comfort zone. I try to make my talks as informative as possible regarding what it's like to be a freelance illustrator, and talk about all the things I wish I had known when I started. I love sharing my experience and answering any questions that aspiring illustrators have, although there are still a lot of things that I'm figuring out myself. Public speaking is a good opportunity to look back, take stock and reflect on your achievements.

Some of the most rewarding experiences I've had came from the feeling you get when you end up being able to do something by yourself. Like the figurines I have created for example, I didn't really know what I was doing and I tried finding ways to collaborate with brands or production companies that could help in the process. In the end, I had to figure a lot of things out by myself, and it meant I learnt along the way. From finding the right 3D designer, manufacturer, printer and marketing it the right way. I say by myself, but I actually had some help from my husband.

Having my first solo show was also a great achievement. For me, it was a personal goal I had when I first moved to London and saw amazing artists having complete freedom in exhibiting their personal work – it was incredible. So when I had my exhibition 'Nobody's Baby', both in Paris and London, it felt really good. And to see everyone turning up and being supportive was very heart-warming.

> "If you feel no restriction in what you're creating, your work will be better and you will be more motivated – so make sure you're doing what you enjoy."

My advice to young designers is to find their own voice. Figure out what really inspires you, and what you love illustrating the most and make that a core base for your style. If you feel no restriction in what you're creating, your work will be better and you will be more motivated – so make sure you're doing what you enjoy. There's never a bad time to change what you do. At the end of the day, the only person you should be worried about is yourself and being proud of your achievements.

Converse
Series of illustrations made
in collaboration with Converse.
The artwork was made into
stickers and printed patterns
to customise the shoes.

Creating these stickers for Converse
was a lot of fun. The brief was very open
and it echoed very well with my work
and the message behind it. There are
some projects that feel like such a good
fit, this was one of them.

Bravery
Pro bono project made with
Australian headscarf brand
Bravery, with part of the profits
going towards Cancer Research.

I love working on projects that transform the artwork into a supportive object, like this scarf for Bravery. It gives the artwork a deeper purpose and the idea of improving someone's mood because of it is very inspiring.

Levi's
Illustration created for a Levi's social campaign promoting their new products.

Marylou Faure

I've worked on a lot of editorial projects
throughout the years, and I love the
exercise of having to sum up a whole
article into a single visual. It's a good way
to practice telling a story in the simplest
and most striking way you can.

Twin Love
An illustration about love
and complicity.

Marylou Faure

Balance for Better
Illustration, made in
collaboration with Grand
Matter, about gender equality.

Home is Where
Pro bono illustration made
to support End of Youth
Homelessness.

The pro bono projects I've been a part of have helped me produce the artwork I love the most. There is always so much freedom in the brief and meaning behind it, that it drives me to create pieces that will really stand out.

Spotify
A series of visuals made for Spotify's first ever illustrated campaign. The illustrations were used for Spotify's social media and OOH advertising in Germany.

Each illustration was animated and had to have a sense of movement and liveliness.

Nike – Netball
Series of illustrations supporting the Netball World Cup.
Each design was used to create patches, t-shirts and posters.

I love the energy and dynamism of this series made for Nike. It allowed me to create characters in a different way, portraying a feeling of speed and movement.

Nike – Sports Bra
Series of illustrations made
for the Nike App, promoting
the use and value of having
a good sport bra.

117

Nike – Women's Football
Series of illustrations made into
a sticker set for the Women's
Football World Cup, supporting
the French team. The stickers
were embroidered and used
to customise the French Kit.

Quartz
Series of illustrations going
alongside Quartz's series called
'How We'll Win', exploring
the fight for gender equality.

It's always refreshing to work on projects
that are shining a light on the issues I
care about, like gender equality and equal
pay. This one was made for Quartz and
it went alongside genuine and interesting
articles about how to make a change.